Kentucky Folklore

original edition 1901 by Sadie F. Price
The Journal of American Folklore,
Vol. 14, No. 52

new edition 2017
edited by John C Ramsey

KENTUCKY FOLKLORE

ON numerous botanical collecting trips through Southern Kentucky, I have found that there still prevail many of the superstitious ideas of a less civilized age. Implicit faith is placed in signs, or "to- kens" (as one quaint old woman termed them), omens and charms, even by very sensible, well-informed people.

One wonders what the schoolmaster has been about all these years, or whether, despite his efforts, these ideas are bound to survive and always retain a niche in the minds of sensible people.

Many of the ideas given below are common to people of other States, but the greater part of them are peculiar to this section, and have probably never before appeared in print.

Following are some of the weather proverbs I have heard here:-

Fruit is never killed by frost in March. Nor is it killed during the light of the moon.

Remove your flannels on the first day of May, and you will not take cold.

If locusts (cicadas) are noisy, it is a sign of dry weather.

Whirlwinds of dust are a sign of dry weather.

It never rains at night during July.

If the sun shines while it is raining, it will rain again the following day.

There will be frost just three months after the first katydid is heard.

Birds and hens singing during rain indicate fair weather.

If roosters crow when they go to roost, it is a sign of rain.

When the coal smoke and gas puffs out into the room with a singing noise, it is a sign of snow.

The first thunder in the spring awakens the snakes.

A common expression when the first robin is seen in the spring is: "You '11 be looking through glass (ice) windows yet!"

The sun always shines brightly some time on Friday and Saturday.

If the weather clears off during hours of darkness, it will rain again in thirty-six hours.

When chickens get on the fence during a rain and pick themselves, it is a sign of clear weather.

When the rain gets thick and heavy, almost like mist, it will turn cold.

If a rainbow bows over a house, there will be a death in that house.

Stretch a yarn string over beans and other young plants in the early spring, and they will not be injured.

The frost will collect on the yarn, and the plants will not be touched.

It always rains for five days in succession after an eclipse of the sun.

If a "Bob-white" only says "Bob " once (that is, does not repeat the first note), there will be rain.

Cool weather in May is called "blackberry winter;" and if it is cool when the dogwood blooms, it is styled "dogwood winter."

If taken sick any time in March that has two new moons, the patient will die.

When the rain-drops stand on the trees, it will rain again. When they drop off, it will stop raining.

It always clears off at milking-time.

It never rains as hard at three o'clock in the afternoon.

"Rain from the east rains three days at

least."

If the sun sets in a cloud on Sunday, it will rain before Wednesday. If on Wednesday, it will rain before Sunday.

Many gnats and flies are a sign of rain.
If the clouds open before seven and shut up again, it will rain be- fore eleven.

"Open and shet is a sign of wet."

If the stars are thick, it is a sign of rain.

If dark clouds arise in the west at sunset and then fall back, it will rain; if they disperse, it will not.

When the peacocks cry a great deal in winter, it is a sign the cold weather is over. When they run along the ground crying, it will rain.

If it rains before seven, it will clear off before eleven.

If there is lightning in the north, it will rain

in twenty-four hours.

Lightning in the south means dry weather.

Three white frosts and then a rain.

The following are some of the ideas entertained, not only by negroes, but by all classes of people, in regard to charm healing:-

A brass ring worn on the left thumb prevents rheumatism.

A leather band worn around the wrist prevents cramp.

To have your ears pierced, or to wear earrings, prevents sore eyes. (It is not unusual to see countrymen and negro men wearing ear- rings.)

To cure a bone-felon, have a person, who, before he was seven years old, has held a mole till it died, hold the finger for one half hour.

For warts, steal a dish-rag and hide it in a stump.

Also, pick the wart with a needle, and put the blood on a piece of paper, then hide this till the paper decays, when the wart will disappear.

Still an- other is to put the blood on a grain of corn, - in the crease at the side of the grain, - and feed it to a fully grown chicken. Also to spit on the wart, and rub it seven times upward with the finger while one chants a hocus-pocus rhyme.

Another cure is to tie as many knots in a string as there are warts, and bury it under a stone.

Warts are thought to be caused by handling a toad.

If a person who has never seen his own father will look in the mouth of a child who has the thrush it will effect a cure.

It is said that in the mountains intelligent

women take their babies miles on horseback, through heat or cold, to have some one, who has never seen his father, blow in their mouths for the thrush.

Rheumatism is treated with pole-cat grease, or red-worm oil.

March snow, or bottled snow-water, is used for sore eyes; and a snail, or slug, is placed on the gum for the toothache. An old woman, with great earnestness, told -me of this last remedy, and also added, "(If you take a 'Bess-bug' (a large black beetle) and cut off his head one drop of blood will flow, this will cure the earache every time."

For toothache a "faith doctor" wrote the following words, " galla, gaffa, gassa," on the wall. With a nail he pointed at each letter of the words, at the same time asking the sufferer if the tooth felt any better. When he reached a letter where the tooth was said to be better he drove the nail in and the tooth ceased aching.

To "take out fire" (cure burns) he wet his

forefinger with spittle, and gently rubbed over the burned places, repeating some "ceremony."

To cure bots in horses, he rubbed the animal nine times from the tip of its nose to the end of the tail, repeating some lingo, then slapped the horse on the side. When this story was told to me, it was added that "the horse would be up and eating grass in half an hour." It is believed that if a man teaches a man this "ceremony," he will lose his power to cure; but he can teach a woman the words.

To stop hemorrhages, this same " faith doctor" has a second per- son repeat, with the patient, the following text from Ezekiel: " And when I passed by thee, and saw thee polluted in thine own blood, I said unto thee, Live."

I have been told by reliable persons that, in the mountains, hemorrhages are checked - or supposed to be- by laying an axe under the bed of the patient, and erysipelas by "striking fire" over the patient's head.

Glandular swellings are treated with two-year-old marrow taken from the inferior maxillary of a hog.

Boils are treated with a poultice of mud-dauber's nests.

Sprains are treated with goose-grease.

Chicken-pox is treated with the water in which the feathers of a black chicken are boiled. This is founded on the belief that the disease is contracted from a chicken, and that "the hair of the dog is good for the bite."

For " fallen palate," the hair on top of the patient's head is grasped and pulled " till it pops," the patient at the same time being made to swallow twice.

Toothache is relieved by making the gums bleed and taking the blood on a long cotton string. This is tied around a dogwood-tree at the place where an incision has been made in the bark.

For nose-bleed, a yarn string is worn around

the left little finger, or a certain gristle is taken from a hog's ear and worn as a preventive.

Buckeyes carried in the pocket are a preventive of rheumatism.

Many of the negro superstitions are quite interesting. An old philosopher told me with great gravity: " If you want peppers to grow, you must git mad. My old 'oman an' me had a spat and I went right out and planted my peppahs an' they come right up!" Still another saying is that peppers, to prosper, must be planted by a red-headed, or by a high-tempered, person. The negro also says that one never sees a jay-bird on Friday, for the bird visits his Satanic majesty to "pack kindling" on that day. The three signs in which the negroes place implicit trust are the well-known ones of the ground- hog's appearing above ground on the second of February; that a hoe must not be carried through a house or a death will follow; and that potatoes must be planted in the dark of the moon, as well as all vegetables that ripen in the ground (and that corn must be planted in the light of the moon).

Feed gunpowder to dogs, and it will make them fierce.

A negro will not burn the wood of a tree that has been struck by lightning, for fear that his house will burn, or be struck by lightning.

If a bird flies into a house, it brings bad luck. If a crawfish, or a turtle catches your toes, it will hold on till it thunders.

When a child, I was told by a black nurse that if a bat alights on one's head, it would stay till it thundered. This was so terrifying that even now I have an unnecessary fear of being clutched by a bat.

To make soap, stir it with a sassafras stick, in the dark of the moon.

Snakes will not come about a garden where gourds are grown.

Boil a biscuit with cabbage, and there will be no odor.

When cooking onions, place a pan of water over them, and there will be no odor.

If you kill the first snake you see in the spring, you will over- come all your enemies that year.

You must not cut a baby's nails before it is a year old; you must bite them off.

A ring around the moon indicates bad weather, which will last as many days or begin in as many days as there are stars enclosed in the circle.

Only a fool can grow gourds.

If you burn the bread, your sweetheart is thinking of you.

It is bad luck to have weeds grow about the house.

If you drop the dish-cloth, it will bring a caller.

It is bad luck not to leave the room by the same door you enter.

Martens go south the fifteenth day of August.

If a young child marks the furniture, it will soon die, - " it is marking itself out of the world."

If a dog howls in front of a house it is a sign of death.

Eat a buckeye and your head will turn round.

The young people in the country can tell you quite as many "signs." Here are a number of them:-

To sit on a table is a sign you wish to marry, while to stumble when going upstairs is a sure sign you will receive a letter.

If your ears burn some one is talking ill of you, while if your hand itches you will receive a present, or shake hands with a stranger.

If your right foot itches, you are to go on a journey; if the left, you are going where you are not wanted.

When your nose itches, some one is coming. If it is when you are away from home, you may know you are wanted at home.

If your right eye itches, you will cry; if the left, you will laugh.

If you sing before breakfast, you will cry before night.

If your apron or shoe comes untied, your sweetheart is thinking of you.

If a bunch of straw comes out of a broom when sweeping, name it and place it over the door, and the person named will call. If the broom falls across the doorway, some one will call.

It is extremely bad luck to step over a broom; if you do this, you must immediately step over it again backwards.

If a bride drops the wedding ring before or during the ceremony, it is a bad omen.

One must not give a friend a knife or other sharp instrument, as it "cuts love."

A common thing with young girls, when they spend their first night in a room, is to name each of the four corners for as many beaux. The corner first looked at in the morning will bear the name of the accepted suitor.

You must not turn a log of wood over in the fire, or you will have bad luck; and if a chunk falls down, you must not turn it around when you replace it. If you spit on it, and name it for your sweet- heart when you replace it, he will come ere it burns out.

If the fire roars, there will be a quarrel in the family.

If two hens fight, two ladies will call.

Catch a butterfly, and bite its head off, and you will have a dress the color of the butterfly; while, if you find a " measuring-worm " (caterpillar) on your dress, you will have a new garment of the same color.
If you see a hairy caterpillar (called "fever-worms" in some sections of the country), spit on it, and it will save you a spell of fever.

"Where the spider webs grow, no beaux don't go."

If you can make your first and little finger meet over the back of the hand, you will marry.

Count ninety-nine white horses and a white mule, and the first person you shake hands with you will marry.

Spit over your little finger when you see a white horse, and your wish will come true.

Look at a new moon over your left shoulder, and make this wish,--

New moon, new, Let me see
Who my future husband is to be;
The color of his hair,
The clothes he is to wear,
And the happy day he is to wed me.

The new moon must never be seen through the trees when making a wish.

A custom known as "sweating eggs" is as follows: Place an egg in front of an open fire at night, and sit in front of it without speaking. Your future "to be" will come in and turn the egg when it is hot. Of course, many pranks are often played on the credulous.

A "dumb supper" is sometimes given. Not a word is spoken by the guests or the hostess during the entire evening. That night, each one who fails to speak will dream of his or her "intended."

The night of the 30th of April spread a handkerchief in a wheat field, and in the morning the name of your future husband or wife will be written in the corner.

Hold a looking-glass over a spring early in the morning of the first day of May, and you will see your future sweetheart's face reflected in the water.

When paring an apple, if the paring does not break, throw it over your left shoulder, and it will form the last initial of your sweetheart's name.

Beat up an egg and add as much salt as you can, stir and eat this before going to bed, and you will dream of your sweetheart, who will come and bring you a drink of water.

If a butterfly comes into the house, a lady will call wearing a dress the color of the butterfly.

When you see the first star in the evening, repeat the following rhyme, then spit over your left shoulder,
and your wish will come true:-

> Star light,
> Star bright!
> The very first star

I have seen to-night,
I wish I may, I wish I might
Have the wish I wish to-night.

When you see the first robin in the spring, sit down on a rock, take off your left stocking, turn it wrong side out; if you find a hair in it, your sweetheart will call to see you. (A negro superstition)

If a rabbit, or squirrel, runs from the right across the road in front of you, it is a sign of good luck; if from the left, you will have bad luck.

If you see grains of corn in the road, company will come; and if you cover them over, it will be a stranger who comes.

In moving, you must not take a cat or a broom.

You will have bad luck if you mend a garment while wearing it, unless you hold a straw in your mouth.

If, in planting corn, you skip a row, there

will be a death in the family.

If a lightning-bug comes into the house, there will be one more or one less to-morrow, - some one will go or some one come.

If you knock down a mud-dauber's nest, you will break your dishes.

When combing your hair, if the comb falls behind you, it is a sign of trouble.

To sneeze at the breakfast table is a sign of death; and to sneeze before breakfast is a sign you will see your sweetheart before Saturday night.

It is bad luck to bring fire where there is fire (coals from another fire), or to have a black cat follow you, or to kill a cat. A woman told me, with great earnestness, that her brother killed a cat, and the next day he found that a valuable mule (one he expected to sell that day for two hundred dollars) had " hung hisself in a grapevine, so he never killed no more cats."

The same woman believes that May butter will make ointment that will cure any ill, and that it never grows rancid.

I have heard the expression, "Wide thumbs will spin gold" (make or earn gold).

To dream of muddy water is a sign of trouble, and of clear water, the reverse.

To dream of the dead is to hear from the living.

Many people of education and refinement believe in these last signs, as well as many others, and though apparently ashamed of them, yet would not think of violating them. There are many families who believe that certain dreams are peculiar to themselves. Thus, a lady believes that to dream of a certain pearl brooch she owns is followed by a death in the family. Another says that a dream of runaway horses is followed by trouble.

The superstitions in regard to the number thirteen, and about beginning a journey or a piece of work on Friday, are, of course, generally believed.

A common saying is that you must not watch a friend out of sight, or you will never see him again.

If one starts away, and turns back, he must sit down, or make a cross mark, before leaving again.

If two persons utter the same word at the same moment, they must lock little fingers, and, without speaking, make a wish.

I have known persons to wear a garment all day that they had put on wrong side out rather than to reverse the luck by changing it.

If you break a mirror, you will have seven years' bad luck; and if you let a baby under a year old look in a mirror, it will die.

If you drop a knife or scissors so that they stand in the floor, it is a sign some one is coming.

You must not place your bed with the head to the west, as that is the way they bury the dead.

If two persons are walking together, they must not let a third pass between them, or go on opposite sides of a tree, or they will have a "falling out."

If you sit in the sun, and look at a yellow caterpillar, you will have a chill.

If you find an Indian arrow, put it in the chimney, and the hawks will not kill the chickens.

Locust-trees are more often struck by lightning than any others.

Fishermen think it brings bad luck to step over the pole, and to spit on the bait brings good luck.

A common saying is:

Wind from the south, hook in the mouth;
Wind from the east, bite the least;

Wind from the north, further off;
Wind from the west, bite the best.

The posts of a rail fence will sink in the ground if not set in the dark of the moon. A house should be shingled in the dark of the moon. A man said that he cut some shingles, and piled them in the woods to weather. He shingled one half of the barn in the light

of the moon, and finished the other side in the dark of the moon, "the light side ripped up (warped), while the dark did not."

You must sow cotton and cabbage seed the 9th of May, and turnip seed the 25th of July.

Plant cotton among your cucumber plants, and insects will not attack your cucumbers.

Place corn-bread crumbs about your cucumber plants. It will attract the ants, and these will destroy the cucumber bugs.

Mulberries are poisonous during the time of the seventeen-year locust.

Hogs fed on apples make the sweetest meat, and when fed on beechnuts, the meat is all fat.

Place a horse-hair in water, and it will turn into a worm.

I save the most ridiculous till the last:

If the inmates of a rat-infested house will write the name of some person on a piece of paper well greased with lard, and put it where the rats get it, - telling them where they will find a better larder, they will forsake this house, and go to that mentioned in the paper.

This is so generally believed in one section of the state (and that, too, in quite an enlightened section), that it was the cause of a bitter neighborhood feud.